Saving and Spending

Tessa Hallenbeck

Consultants

Shelley Scudder
Gifted Education Teacher
Broward County Schools

Caryn Williams, M.S.Ed.
Madison County Schools
Huntsville, AL

Publishing Credits

Dona Herweck Rice, *Editor-in-Chief*

Lee Aucoin, *Creative Director*

Torrey Maloof, *Editor*

Diana Kenney, M.A.Ed., NBCT,
Associate Education Editor

Marissa Rodriguez, *Designer*

Stephanie Reid, *Photo Editor*

Rachelle Cracchiolo, M.S.Ed., *Publisher*

Image Credits: Cover & pp. 1, 5 Corbis; pp. 9, 16, 24 Alamy; pp. 12, 18–19 Getty Images; p. 14 The Granger Collection; p. 10 The Library of Congress [LC-H814-T01-1006]; p. 6 The Library of Congress [LC-USF33-020774-M3]; pp. 8, 17 ThinkStock; p. 21 (top) Diana Kenney; All other images from Shutterstock.

Teacher Created Materials

5301 Oceanus Drive
Huntington Beach, CA 92649-1030
http://www.tcmpub.com

ISBN 978-1-4333-6977-3

Table of Contents

DONATION

Up to You

You make **decisions** (dih-SIZH-uhnz) every day. You decide what to wear. You decide what to eat. When you have money, you decide how to spend it. It is up to you.

A girl decides what to wear.

A boy decides what to eat.

The Power to Buy

Money can buy **goods**. Goods are things you can touch and hold. Books and toys are goods. Money can also buy **services** (SUR-vis-iz). Services are things people can do for you. Cleaning and cooking are services.

Toys are goods.

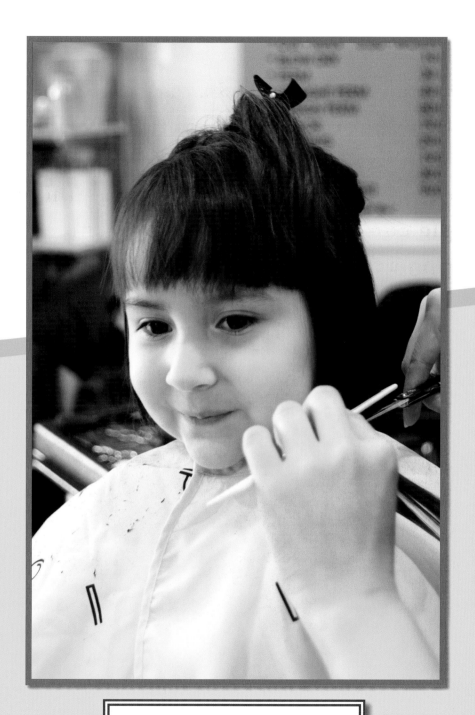

A haircut is a service.

Goodbye, Money!

When you **buy** things, you give up your money. You **trade** it for something else.

A boy buys a toy truck.

A woman's dog helps her shop.

Buying things is a choice. But sometimes it is a **necessary** (NES-uh-ser-ee) choice. It is smart to buy things you need.

People buy food in 1935.

That Looks Cool!

Ads on TV can be tricky. They try to get kids to buy things they do not need.

This TV ad tries to get kids to buy a toy truck.

Sometimes, buying things is not necessary. You may buy things you want but do not need. You make a choice. What will happen if you buy things you want? Will you have enough money for things you need?

A doll is something you want.

Food is something you need.

Hello, Choices!

Most people cannot buy all the things they want. They have to choose. They think about what they want and need. They think about how much money they have. They decide what they can **afford**.

A family buys frozen custard in 1939.

Bad Timing

Bad choices are often made late in the day. The brain is too tired to think clearly.

This family is tired after a long day of shopping.

Even if you can afford what you want or need, wait. Ask yourself questions. Can you make it yourself? Will it last? Candy, for example, is gone once you eat it.

A boy makes a scarf with his grandma to save money.

Tell Me More!

Many people look up goods and services on the Internet. They find out more about what they want before they buy.

A girl shops with her mom on the Internet.

Take Your Time

When you have money, you have decisions to make. You can spend your money. You can save it or **donate** it. Take time to think about your choices. Make a good decision about how to use your money.

These children donate their money to a lady in need in 1939.

Donate It!

When you donate, you give things to help people in need. You can donate time. You can donate money. You can donate things.

This class saves money to donate where it is needed.

Plan It!

When you have money, you must make many choices. Pretend you have $20. What choices will you make? Will you spend it, save it, or donate it? Write about your plan. Tell your parents why you made those choices.

A budget is a plan about what you will do with your money.

Sara's Budget

Monthly allowance	$20
Save	−$10
Buy a toy	−$5
Buy a book	−$5
Amount left	$0

This girl writes about what she will do with her money.

Glossary

afford—to have enough money to pay for things

buy—to pay money for something

decisions—choices

donate—to give things, money, or time to help people in need

goods—things people can buy

necessary—needed

services—work or help for sale

trade—to get something in return for something else

Index

Your Turn!

Make It Yourself

The boy in the photo is making a scarf. It is something he needs. Draw a picture of something you can make. Is it something you want? Is it something you need?